West Cumbria Mining:
The Silence between Shadows

West Cumbria Mining: The Silence between Shadows

David Banning

CHROMA EDITIONS

"The balance of nature is not a status quo; it is fluid, ever shifting, in a constant state of adjustment. Man, too, is part of this balance. Sometimes the balance is in his favour; sometimes — and all too often through his own activities — it is shifted to his disadvantage"

Rachel Carson — *Silent Spring*

00:01

We lived at Devonshire Road in the small resort of St Annes, on the Fylde coast in Lancashire. A cut-through just a stone's throw away from our red brick semi led onto a sandy beach flanked by dunes at the edge of the big brash jungle that was Blackpool. The residential nexus at Lytham formed a quieter association further south, merging somewhere along Clifton Drive's parade of suburban flush and luxury retirement homes. A treat we all looked forward to was the 'annual razzle dazzle,' a special night-time ride along the Golden Mile in the back of my father's blue Viva estate. A tradition rooted in the days when coal was the future, after Victorian industry had dubbed the new electricity 'artificial sunshine' due to the arrival of electric street lighting.

Electricity that used dial-boards to make connections (like an original form of switchboard) while the dark stuff stoked engines and boilers. I remember calling my father's car 'Viv' after Ade Edmondson's punk character Vivian from *The Young Ones*, a favourite TV show at the time. The car's all-British severe, razor-edge lines and spacious interiors were built by Vauxhall at an old airstrip between the Manchester Ship Canal and the river Mersey, at what became known as the Ellesmere Port factory. *For you, for life…* With above-average roominess, Viv afforded us a grandstand view of the illuminations, 10 kilometres of shimmering luminescence; an electrical feast where you could even have your own name in lights! Illuminating history for over 140 years, after the humble beginning of just 8 arc lights on 60ft poles that shone down on the promenade.

More recently, after crowds were excluded from the annual switch-on (due to Covid restrictions), Blackpool Council confirmed a shorter dissolve to a greener energy source.

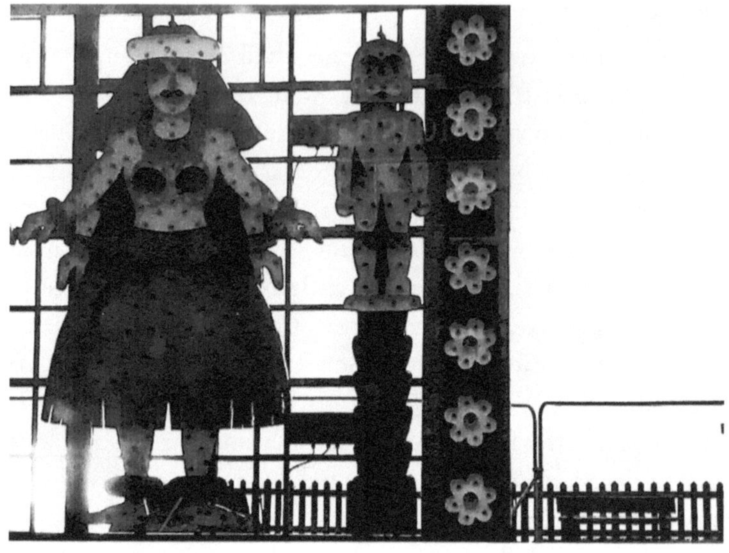

The future would be powered by renewables made up of wind and solar energy, with a firm pledge to kick a coal habit stretching back hundreds of years. Going net-zero by 2030 to embed the narrative of the past in the present moment…

00:02

I lay awake for most of the night listening to the winds sprawling back and forth, as yet another storm with the fury of an angry mob trembled like a grim tattoo. Unchecked in the tremors of nature's beating heart, danger ebbed and flowed. Just like at the start of lockdown, all of us confined inside again. Coiled up on armchairs or beds the cats weren't impressed, looking up now and again with a sulky indifference. From a smeared print snapped at Devonshire Road years ago, my great uncle Sam stared out from the centre of the picture. Behind him in the background was a pink rose bush and beyond that some white iron gates at the end of a long driveway.

In such moments of pure contemplation Susan Sontag wrote, "To take a photograph is to participate in another person's (or thing's) mortality, vulnerability, mutability…All photographs testify to time's relentless melt." During the clear out of my mother's place on the south coast, I'd found a box full of family photos underneath a bent and buckled shelf at the bottom of a hallway cupboard. Retirement in the late nineties led to the chalk white cliffs of Saltdean, a small suburb on the eastern edge of Brighton and Hove after my father had left his advisory role with the Post Office. In a place full of villa-like homes and renowned for its jaunty deco air, both parents became keen supporters of the listed Saltdean Lido Community Centre, an art deco masterpiece designed by R.W.H. Jones. Using streamlined forms and ocean-liner inspired details, the British architect also designed the iconic Grand Ocean Hotel, a flotilla of glitz and sophistication epitomising the Modern Movement's *architecture of pleasure.*

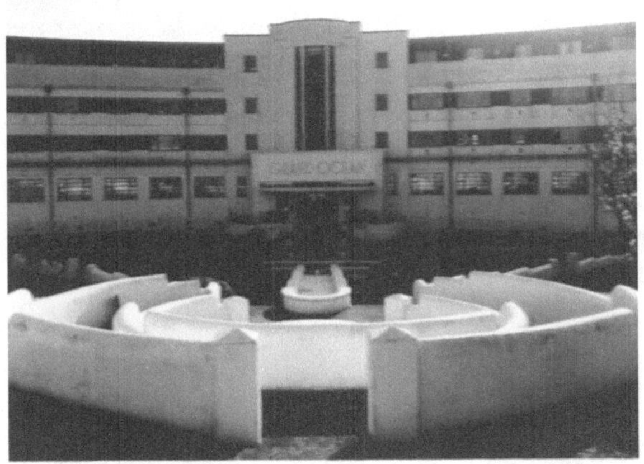

By October 1941 though, the national war effort's Auxiliary Fire Service had requisitioned the hotel for use as a training college. Amidst the political and social upheaval of post-war reconstruction, Billy Butlin bought and restored the near-derelict building, lavishing it with modern day luxuries such as 'television theatres' and 'constant hot water.' In the permissive Sixties, thousands of holidaymakers rolled up for fun in the sun, with Butlins promising a "Continental-style sea-side resort hotel with glass-enclosed sun-decks – a sunbather's paradise!" The Grand Leisure Group eventually took over the former 'honeymoon hotel' around the same time my parents moved into the area. Not long afterwards, the dark dials of decay closed the hotel doors forever. Nearby, new waves picked out the bones from whispers spreading rumours of in-duction centres housing asylum seekers. Lurking with intent, the localist and cosmopolitan discourse formed a barrier of memory charting the rise of the far right across the UK and Europe. A nostalgic recollection fuelled by protest votes draw-ing on anti-immigration scaremongering. For years, the Grand Ocean remained sad and forlorn at its lookout over the shingle and longshore drift, until a £43 million development project funded by Explore Living turned the Grade-II listed structure into luxury apartments. Whirring in the English Channel and wavering between profit and loss, a cleaner future brought the installation of 116 wind turbines along the south coast from East Worthing to Brighton.

Emerging from the darkness, movements of currents on and offshore were now framed by the withered stumps of time. Once more, I pressed sleepless fingertips onto the centre of the picture, where the blurred lines of my great uncle's ghost gazed off to the side. Beneath the music ahead of his shape, the gradual dissolution of life drifted down into the silence between shadows.

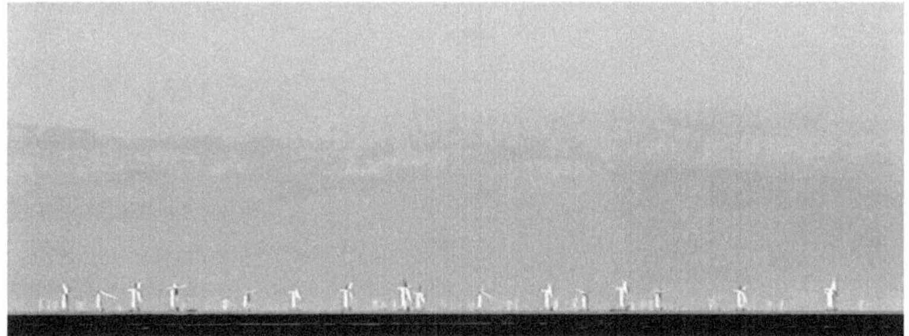

00:03

Sam Snaith was born in 1910 at Great Broughton in the Bridekirk parish, below Derwent Ward, once part of the historic county of Cumberland. The 1911 census shows his father Jacob Snaith, a 38 year old miner, living in three rooms with a wife, three sons and two daughters. In 1901, Great and Little Broughton had a population that had grown to 1,334 mainly due to the expansion of mining on Broughton Moor since the 1860s (Buckhill colliery opened in 1873) until the site was used for munitions storage from the late 1930s before its eventual closure in the early 1990s. With Coal Measures formed from superimposed cyclothems of shale, siltstone, coal and sandstone, several intersecting fault sets traversed an area that displayed evidence of significant post-glacial erosion.

At the turn of the twentieth century, Sam's father Jacob lived at Ash Tree Farm, Little Broughton, with brothers Thomas and John and a sister named Hannah. The men of the household, like Sam's grandfather George, (at the age of 62), worked either as a Coalminer hewer or labourer in several pits on the neighbouring Whitehaven coast.

CENSUS OF ENGLAND AND WALES, 1911.

Before writing on this Schedule please read the Examples and the Instructions given on the other side of the paper, as well as the headings of the Columns. The entries should be written in full.

Number of Schedule 242 (To be filled up by the Enumerator when collecting.)

The contents of the Schedule will be treated as *confidential*. Strict care will be taken that no information is disclosed with regard to individual persons. The returns are not to be used for proof of age, as in connection with Old Age Pensions, or for any other purpose than the preparation of Statistical Tables.

NAME AND SURNAME	RELATIONSHIP to Head of Family	AGE (last Birthday) and SEX		PARTICULARS as to MARRIAGE					PROFESSION or OCCUPATION of Persons aged ten years and upwards					BIRTHPLACE of every person.	NATIONALITY of every Person born in a Foreign Country.	INFIRMITY.
		Ages of Males	Ages of Females	Condition as to Marriage	Completed years the present Marriage has lasted	Total Children Born Alive	Children still Living	Children who have Died	Personal Occupation	Industry or Service	Whether Employer, Worker, or Own Account	Whether Working at Home				
1. Jacob Snaith	Head	38		married					Collier Hewer	150	Worker		Cumberland Broughton	British	
2. Mary Snaith	wife		35	do		8	5	5					Gt Broughton	British subjects Cumb	
3. Doris Snaith	daughter		11						School	390			Cockermouth Cumb		
4. Lewis Snaith	son	8											Cockermouth Cumb		
5. George Snaith	son	6											Cockermouth Cumb		
6. Blanche Snaith	daughter		4										Broughton Cumb		
7. Samuel Snaith	son	1											Broughton Cumb		
8															
9															
10															
11															
12															
13															
14															
15															

(To be filled up by the Enumerator.)

		Total.		
	Males.	Females.	Persons.	
	4	3	7	4

Initials of Enumerator R.T.

(To be filled up by, or on behalf of, the Head of Family or other person in occupation, or in charge of this dwelling.)

Write below the Number of Rooms in this Dwelling (House, Tenement, or Apartment). Count the kitchen as a room but do not count scullery, landing, lobby, closet, bathroom; nor warehouse, office, shop.

3

I declare that this Schedule is correctly filled up to the best of my knowledge and belief.

Signature *Jacob Snaith*

Postal Address *Little Broughton, Cockermouth*

They dug coal out of land owned by Hugh Cecil Lowther, the 5th Earl of Lonsdale, the so called 'Yellow Earl' due to a fondness for the colour on his cars and livery. A pleasure seeker, who gained enormous wealth from the proceeds of the family coal mines in the west of Cumberland and best known as first president of the National Sporting Club. Standing high above Whitehaven harbour on dramatic sandstone cliffs, Haig Pit (supposedly named after the controversial Field Marshal dubbed 'The Butcher of the Somme'), became the last deep coal mine sunk on Lonsdale's land. After the war, Britain's victory heralded Haig as a national hero. With the euphoria that followed, a large bronze equestrian sculpture in Whitehall and several other celebratory statues depicting him were erected up and down the land.

Over time though, opinions hardened and dissenting voices emerged throughout the Great Depression, wondering what they had fought for. One of several poems in response to the brutality and loss, Wilfred Owen's *Anthem for Doomed Youth* with its 'shrill, demented choirs of wailing shells' signalled a more sceptical and moral stance than any glorifying statues could instil. Even wartime Prime Minister David Lloyd George took a swipe at Haig in his memoirs: 'I have never met any man in high position who was so utterly devoid of imagination.' And whilst the War's consequences continue to shape our world today, remnants of the lost generation can only salute stone images in a dream kingdom of death, where wailing shells call to them from sad, unmarked graves.

00:04

There were 43 Cumberland collieries being worked in 1900, reduced to just 25 by 1938. When Sam entered the voids armed with a pick and shovel the Cumberland coalfields were largely dependent upon the local iron and steel industry and its demands for coke. About one-third of all output was converted into coke for use in local furnaces. Sam avoided conscription during the Second World War, but a shortage of miners coupled with absenteeism led to a fall in productivity throughout Cumberland. The post-war period of extreme suffering, high unemployment and widespread human misery marked the beginning of a slow burn of decline for West Cumberland. A former prosperous district turned into an economic wasteland due to an excessive dependence on coal. The lamps of my ancestors like most other families from the area viewed mining as a largely hereditary occupation with many ex-miners simply unaware of any career away from the pit.

Despite a total lack of opportunities or encouragement to retrain, Sam eventually moved to a modest white bungalow on the edge of the small market town of Cockermouth, birthplace of the poet Wordsworth and his sister Dorothy and a couple of miles from his own. He lived there alone with a trusty alsatian, scatching a living from house clearances until the end of his life. Inside the property, there were dimly lit rooms and bare walls, but from a lounge window, far off, I remember catching a glimpse of Skiddaw's nobler magnificence shrouded in cloud. This lasting memory was from my one and only childhood visit to his bungalow. It was a Sunday afternoon after my father had loaded us all into Viv again. From one unheated room to another, right through the hall and passageway, stuff was crammed-in everywhere, spilling out onto the sloping driveway and even among the grey leaves of the silver birch trees beyond the garden gate. A spoil tip formed out of a motley assortment of furniture and bric-a-brac that nevertheless my great uncle seemed to know intimately.

Sensing a kindred spirit, we talked about the magpies who stole eggs from a blackbird's nest in honeysuckle by the back door and how on occasion, the wonderful sight of a heron flying overhead contrasted with the noisy skirmishes of sparrows protecting their patch. Sam described sitting in the stillness at dusk under a low slated roof watching rooks and jackdaws gather in a raucous whirring of wings, a steady migration to the nearby farmland woods. 'Wait there a minute!' he said, before disappearing briefly to rummage through a chest of drawers that half-blocked the kitchen door. As rain crashed down, I followed him down the hallway and stopped briefly to peer at an intimidating cream coloured enamelled hunk. Opposite the Aga's multiple doors were several tins of dog food, a bundle of small twigs and a pile of letters spread across a wooden table next to a windowsill covered in slate chippings and sandstone pebbles. Suddenly Sam stopped searching and turned to me triumphantly.

'Look! I was wonderin' where these were.' He gave a throaty laugh while holding aloft a pair of antique binoculars with a matching leather case. 'Might be worth a bit now you know'. At the exact same moment his dog barked and jumped up, while a clap of thunder shook the bungalow.

00:05

As a teenager I used to idle away a lot of spare time on the dunes, often amongst the kind of wind and rain that could take your breath away. Nature in its raw. Smooth exotic deserts towering above homes and beach walkers rising up to some 50 feet and covering around 200 acres between Blackpool and Lytham. Over 9000 years in the making, an enormous beach with a wide tidal range. A natural sea defence and rich wildlife habitat formed by obstacles trapped in sand and reinforced by the growth of grasses like Lyme or the fast-growing Marram grass. During storms, this pre-emptive combination can help reduce the risk of floods by absorbing the energy of the Irish Sea and releasing sand to lessen wave action. Throughout a long career, the painter L.S. Lowry often returned to the Fylde coast to sketch and paint these local seascapes.

Distinguished art critics would later pour praise on them. So did his mother, who apparently never really cared much for the more renowned industrial scenes of 'match-stalk men and match-stalk cats and dogs'. Retrospectively, it appears several of the seascapes shared the same title of *Yachts at Lytham*, including my own framed print that has decorated the walls of a succession of rental properties for the last 10 years or so. With sea and sky merging into one, the shimmering light of the water juxtaposed against the colour and movement of the boats has always conveyed a sense of childhood nostalgia to me. I would later discover it was a copy of his mother's favourite painting of the Fylde coast, which hung on the artist's bedroom wall until he died aged 88 in 1976.

Armed with a battered copy of the RSPB Handbook of the Seashore, I would try and emulate the nineteenth century poet John Clare and 'drop down' amongst the grass clumps on the dunes at St. Annes. Lingering to admire what I discovered were such curiosities as yellow flowered Isle of Man cabbage and dune helleborne orchids or more common plants like sea holly, dune pansies and even the odd flowering dandelion. Grayling butterflies and burnet moths weaved lightly among the plants, while I made good use of Sam's old binoculars to follow the curves and freedoms of the rising larks or encircling hawks. He always claimed they were British World War I issue, and a recent look on eBay backed-up his assertions. There were similar looking pairs with bodies covered in black leather that featured central focus wheels and fixed frames with factory set eye pieces. All of them French made, under the generic name of the 'War Office Pattern.'

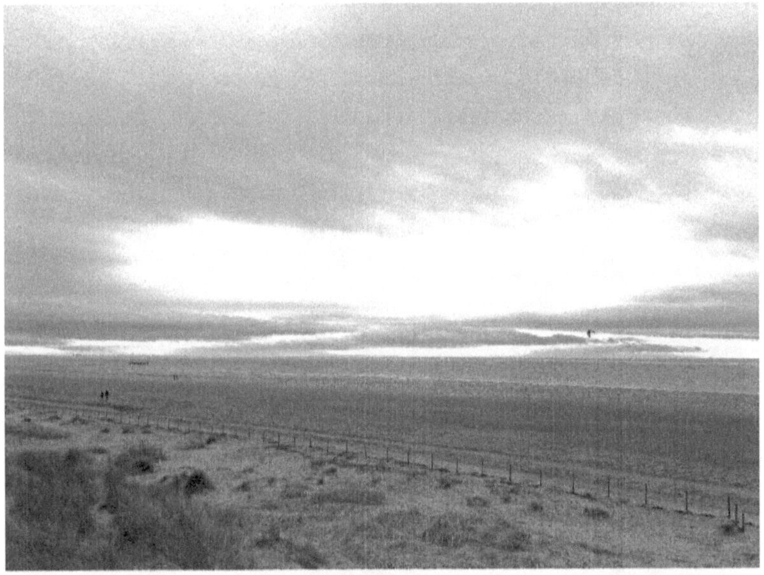

Over the past 150 years, 80% of the Fylde's sand dunes have been lost to development and erosion. Removed from their natural environment, deserted landscapes drift away into an abyss. In the coastal defence game management of properties and roads, nothing is left behind in the so-called process of evolution. I remember sometimes crawling into the sloping hollows sculpted next to the labyrinth of dune paths, trying to escape the buffeting of fierce gales rattling in off the Irish Sea. Thankfully though, on more tranquil days, the same sloping hollows became a carpet of sand, where I could lie down and enjoy the flaring music of gulls and crows crisscrossing the ridges above. With their distinctive cries ringing in my ears, the landscaped gardens of several beachfront properties provided useful reference points when swinging my antique binoculars into place. Other ground nesting birds like linnets and stonechats regularly patrolled the sandy humps too, while sanderlings scampered and probed looking for scraps of crab, fish or jellyfish - those hypnotic creatures that pulse like alien life forms in the water. Latent under epic skies, I used to think that I'd been transported back to an earlier age, from the broad expanse of no-man's land to an old Victorian seaside town with miles and miles of shifting sands. At nightfall, with the wind singing in the dark, dances of death filled the sky with ashes dissolving like tears, empty like time itself.

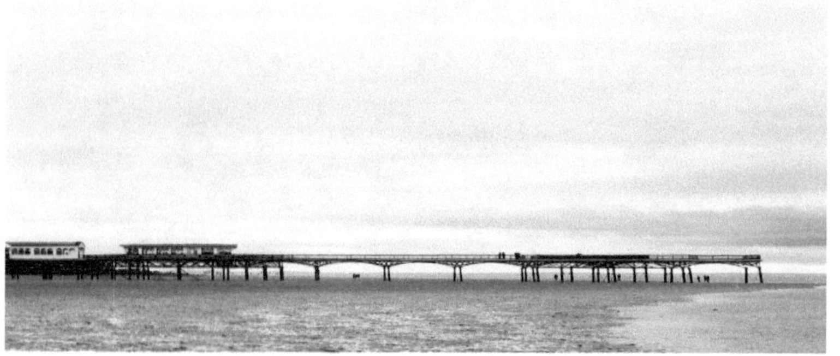

00:06

A few years before the outbreak of the Second World War, George Orwell's left-wing publisher Victor Gollancz commissioned him to write an account of the depressed industrial areas of the North of England. Given the substance of some of Orwell's earlier work, notably, *Down and Out in Paris and in London*, Gollancz must have had an inkling of what he'd let himself in for. After quitting a part-time bookseller role in leafy Hampstead, Orwell spent time away in Lancashire and Yorkshire throughout January and March 1936.

Deeply shocked by the filth and relentless class struggles of capitalist industrialisation, he set about documenting the 'condition of England' upon his return to London. He eventually delivered a manuscript, *The Road to Wigan Pier* in mid-December of that same year. Part social reportage, part socialist polemic, Gollancz felt uneasy about the content of the second half of the text which he thought 'highly provocative'.

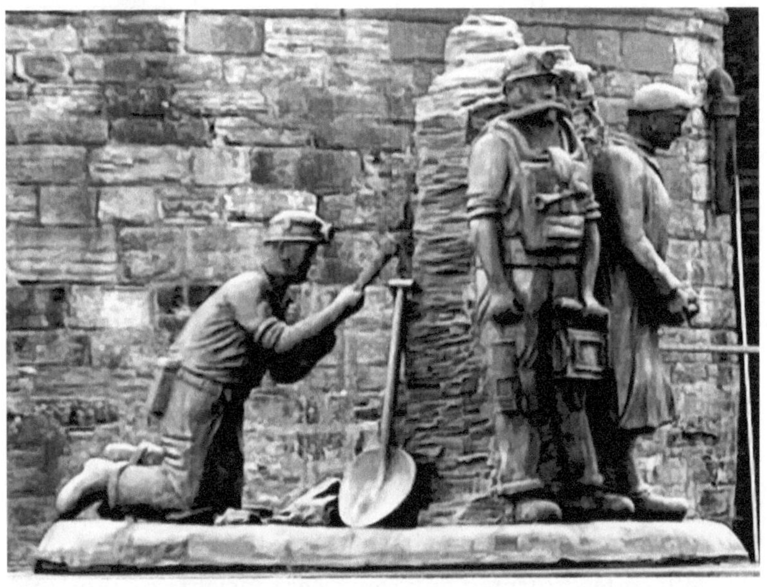

And with Orwell's representatives refusing to allow any cuts, Gollancz responded with a foreword of his own, openly criticising parts of the text for being too self-indulgent. When the book was first published in March 1937, Orwell was away fighting in the Spanish Civil War. Part one, a description of Northern working-class life in the mid-thirties, was also issued separately by the Left Book Club series, which Gollancz had helped found.

Gripping and often perverse, Orwell famously declared the era one in which the coal miner was 'second in importance only to the man who ploughs the soil'. A civilisation founded on coal with the machines that keep us alive and the machines that make the machines dependent on it too. It documented sounds and smells from the clamping of clogs on the cobbled streets to the dusty fiery stench that permeated the works. Miners had to crawl through a circadian road to hell to reach the 4ft high shiny black monolith known as the coal face.

Packed like sardines in a tin can, they were covered from head to foot in a smooth coat of coal dust. The cheapness of human life in our own history, this was the harshest form of manual labour, with half-naked men driving shovels under fallen rocks, while coal was carried away with the deafening roar of the conveyor belt. Poverty and squalor. Child labour. Changing techniques. Stoppages and strikes. Accidents, disasters and fatalities. Working conditions and safety measures. Working five and a half days a week for over fifty hours.

00:07

Sam never spoke directly about his time in the Whitehaven pits. Or indeed offered any significant insights or thoughts surrounding my other ancestors. Although I knew my grandmother Doris Bewley had left the ubiquitous poverty of Great Broughton aged just 17 to join the capital's increasing noise and rush. Sending monies back to Cumberland from her employment as a maid in several plush properties before she married and settled in North London. Curiously, she had used her mother's maiden name on the 1908 National School Admission Register before changing it back to Snaith on the 1911 census. Perhaps this indicated another reason as to why she left Cumberland at such a young age and never returned. From the hewer's pick to Whitehaven's coastal trading fleet, my ancestors were born into a family trade plied by men and boys bred to the job. A filthy job for life, fuelling the industrial revolution with the world's dirtiest fossil fuel. Driving down passages cut through several strata to the surface of the earth. Coal Hewer was the most common occupation attributed to them, although the job title only officially appeared for the first time on the 1901 Census. Enumerators were instructed to start using it in order to differentiate hewers from other miners, and to ensure consistency across the returns.

The title 'Hewer' is actually derived from German: Hauer or Häuer, and refers to miners who worked the seams with a sharpened pick head. On my ancestors' patch, workings were driven deeper and further seawards after 1850. By 1912, Whitehaven's annual output of 513,724 tons made up nearly 25% of Cumberland's as a whole. Much of the coal 'won' by the coastal collieries was raised from workings under the sea. Sometimes they stretched for a couple of miles with the deepest about 150 fathoms below. In a clear testimony to the continued growth of the industry, Ireland provided the largest supply of immigrant workers along with Scots resident in Cumberland and others who came from neighbouring areas such as Westmorland, Lancashire, Yorkshire, Durham and Northumberland.

From the pits to the ports. The coastal strip of West Cumberland was reborn from an isolated, sparsely populated agricultural region into a booming industrial zone. Ships carrying exports to Ireland led to an expansion of the ports at Whitehaven, Workington and Maryport, while deposits of iron ore, coal and limestone soon transformed Workington into a centre for the manufacture of iron and steel.

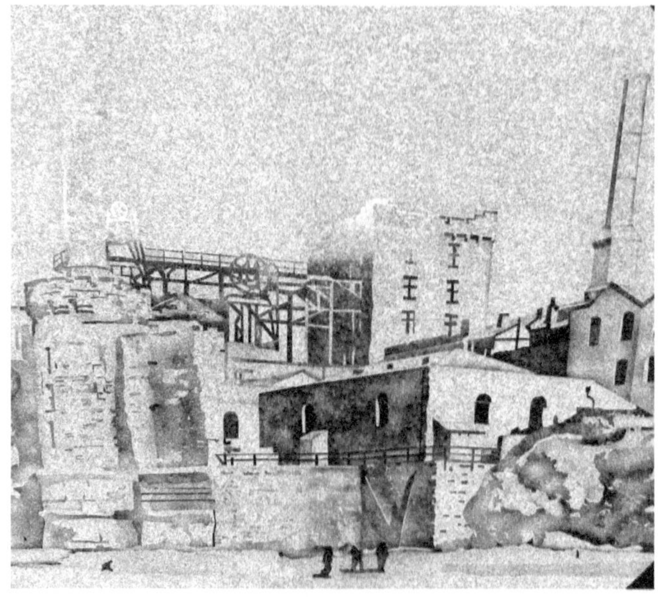

But the boom began to bust with the decline of ship-building in the 1940s, and despite powering much of the world's economies for over three centuries, the age of the first fossil fuel was coming to an end. The coal industry in West Cumberland, as in the rest of the UK, left behind an arresting history of profit, pain and poverty where the mastery of nature ruthlessly exposed gaps between the rich and poor. From this sense of helplessness and lack of justice, strikes became the only weapon available to a workforce hidden away in the depths of the earth.

In April 1984, one month after the titanic clash of the last English civil war began, Sam passed away. He died alone amid an endless collection of clutter in a new world of dread and fear. The miners' strike of 1984/85 would go down in British history as a chillingly brutal affair. One so pivotal it broke the power of the unions and changed society for good.

Intriguingly, looking back almost 40 years after the strike ended, it's still rarely discussed at any length, surprising since its effects were so long term. Thatcher's bruising victory gave birth to a world of personal self-interest and to her supporters, vindicated her notorious denials of the value of 'society'. Rule Britannia had built a wall around flying pickets, police violence, state harassment, debts, betrayals, anger, despair and pride. Controlling the past and the future, the clocks were now striking thirteen. In West Cumbria, the dying coals of Haig Pit were finally extinguished in March 1986, its closure one of many to consign the ailing state-funded industry to the hydrocarbon slag-heap.

00:08

Splashed all over the front pages of the Whitehaven News - Copeland's push to house Small Modular Reactors (SMR's). The "largest engineering collaboration the UK has ever seen". I'd picked up a copy of the paper from the Tesco superstore next to the railway station. With the caption of 'Fact-Finding', a half-smirking local Tory MP viewed the Holy Grail with an excruciatingly smug expression. Powering up, SMR's and new nuclear. Next to a model of the Rolls Royce creation backed by a £195 million cash injection from private investors and a £210 million grant from the Government. Clean, low carbon, affordable energy returning £52 billion to the UK war chest by 2050, with the dark side of Sellafield's talent pool at the forefront of delivering the new economy. Departing the car park under an azure sky of deepest summer, I headed toward the distinctive pyramid shape on top of the Gaiety Cinema. Brand new you're retro; at nearly 100 years old it was revived and refurbished from the early 20th century building in Octo-

ber 2015. Originally one of three, the Gaiety is now the only
survivor after the Queen's Cinema and Empire Theatre hit the
cutting room floor. Passing the royal blue entrances on Tang-
ier Street, a group of five teenagers with glowing tangerine
skin expressed their youth in crop tops and low-rise skirts.
They were being followed by a babble of chancers throwing
chips at one another and decked out in rugby league shirts the
same colour as the cinema doors.

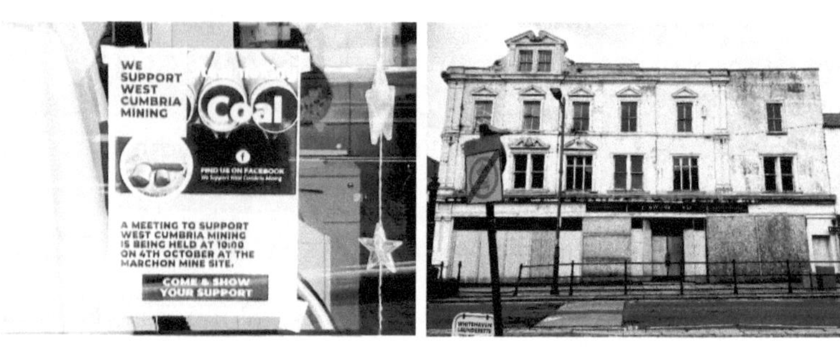

"We Support West Cumbria Mining", a poster posi-
tioned next to a set of Christmas lights caught my eye in the
window of the Civic Hall off Lowther Street. It advertised a
meeting in support of West Cumbria Mining's proposal for a
new state of the art coal mine. There was no other energy on
this side of town though. Shadows old and mastless crept
across rows of pastel-coloured Georgian-style facades bathed
in a faded grandeur. Rounding a corner onto the long silent
sweep of Irish Street towers of scaffolding dwarfed a line of
boarded-up buildings. I couldn't make up my mind if this was
a sign of developers moving in, or proof that years of rigid
reversal need more than a set of rhetorical slogans to fix
things. The light was starting to fade as I walked down King
Street in the direction of one of the oldest remaining coal
wharves in Britain. Moving through a diminishing retail zone,

the effects of the imperishable pandemic were most keenly felt here. Another body blow to a once proud mining town laden with distortions. Transitioned into a dead spot, sterile and increasingly uninhabited. Proud of our past. Energised for our future. Shop Local. Keep it in Copeland. Under the nuclear umbrella, a set of Copeland Borough Council's taglines reflected from a dusty shop front. Mere fragments of broken music disguised as memory.

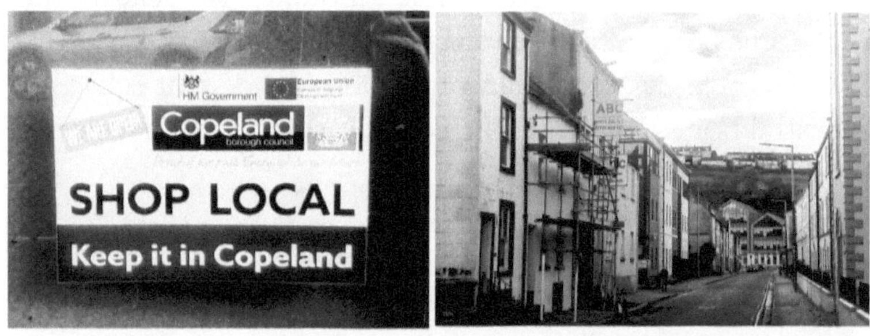

Closing us down, a scattering of large grey and white herring gulls squabbled around the harbour jetty. The site has been turned into a reservation for the feathered bandits who fight like cat and dog over discarded trash and dive-bomb any unsuspecting visitors. By contrast, a small group of sickly-looking younger gulls, mottled brown in colour, emitted peculiar high-pitched whimpers and cast a lingering spell among the silent shadows. Following the waymarkers up to Wellington Pit's impressive ventilation shaft known as the Candlestick, the Cumbria Coastal Way led onto a former wagon track used to shunt coal down to the harbour. A grey coastline made up of coal measures and industrial waste formed a complete contrast to the distinctive red sandstone of the softer St Bees shales some six miles further south. On the cliff top directly outside Haig Pit, a scattered chorus line with varied trappings of cameras, binoculars and tripods had gathered for *Seawatch*. A special event organised by Cumbria Wildlife Trust to gather data for a wildlife survey looking for whales, dolphins and other marine mammals.

I fell into conversation with a gentleman drinking from a flask and wearing regulation black North Face puffer and beige cargo pants. He spoke candidly of his disappointment at the outcome of the global climate conference COP26 that had just ended in Glasgow, while a bouquet of delicate nut-like aromas drifted off toward the perfect mirror of the Irish Sea. In the grey and smoky afternoon, the distant echoes of ancestral bones hacked at the coal measures beneath our feet.

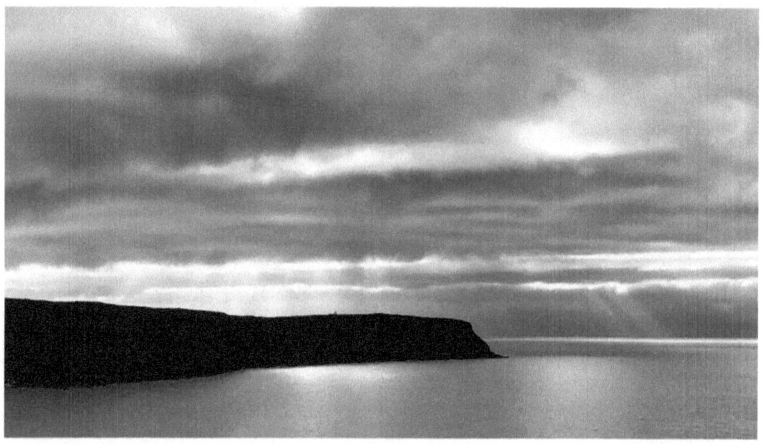

00:09

19 March 2019. At a meeting of the Development Control Committee of Cumbria County Council in Kendal, formal planning approval for the development of the Cumbrian Metallurgical Coal Project – to be known as Woodhouse Colliery, was unanimously granted (subject to 99 planning conditions). Every hand raised in favour prompted cries of 'disgusting'

from environmentalists who attended the vote. The decision to support the first deep coal mine in Britain for thirty years was subsequently ratified after a second unanimous ballot held on 31 October 2019. West Cumbria Mining (WCM), a company committed to operational and environmental excellence.

Great Coal. Great Steel. Great Britain.

Ever since 2014, when WCM announced its plans to create a new coal mine, clashes with environmental groups were inevitable. With a state of the art colliery situated off the Whitehaven coast on the former Marchon chemicals works site, everything seemed poised to progress into the construction phase, after the government's controversial decision not to challenge the initial planning application. As an employer of choice, WCM promised to put an end to the long running saga by offering 500 new jobs underpinned by a zero harm safety culture inspired by the corporate buzzwords *diversity* and *inclusion*. Despite clear claims on their website that the company was privately owned in the UK, a private equity manager EMR Capital (registered in the Cayman Islands) emerged as the parent company owning over 80% of shares. Suddenly fears were provoked over finances, asset-stripping and location of the company offices. Might any future investments be discharged into the world's oceans like the release of radioactive waste? By the sea, arriving in a future imbued with the matter of West Cumbria.

Whitehaven, a town made up of the haves and the have not's, where luxury capitalism and the economic impact of Sellafield contrast sharply with widespread poverty, child depravation and a population in decline. The empty hyperbole of taglines and slogans. *Coal for Steel.* Indigenous versus imported. A plan for jobs. Growing the economy and the much-trailed 'levelling up'. Building back better with wind turbines, cars, trains and nuclear power stations. A new mine for new coking coal to supply the UK steel industry. Feeding hungry mouths in a carbon neutral environment. With the aid of Bolter Miners, Continuous Miners and Roadheader Drivers it would be much better to dig West Cumbrian coal out of the ground instead of somewhere else in the world. Accurate cutting and productivity installing roof supports that help transfer new coal from the machines onto conveyors controlled by drivers in a cab. Drill operators and support miners replacing what was one of the hardest jobs on earth. Mechanisation supplanting the brute force of folk like my ancestors, whose picks and shovels dug holes in the pandemonic depths.

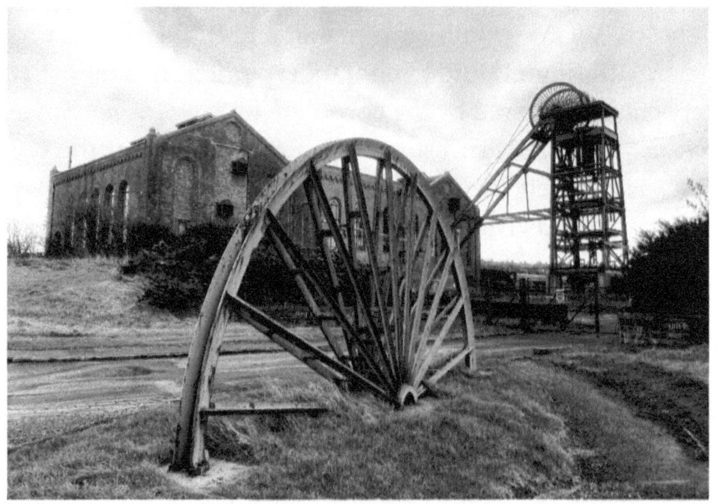

00:10

Before my Dad's health started to decline, he wrote down a list of names on the back of a flyer advertising 'Old Fashioned Bingo Evenings' and told me to keep it safe. These regular Bingo nights were usually held at the Telscombe Civic Centre, a small pyramid shaped complex just off the chocker block coast road running between Brighton and Newhaven.

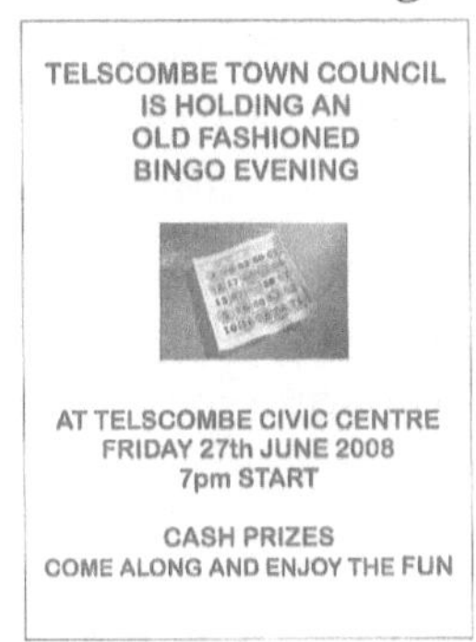

Ahead of the curve after his election as a local councillor, he revived a unique brand of bingo-lingo at a time when the former national pastime seemed to be vanishing for good. With the promise of fun and cash prizes, the evenings soon gained a loyal following, helping to raise respectable amounts for local charities at the same time.

His list, written in capitals with a hard pencil comprised the names of five coal miners from former West Cumberland towns, with William (Billy) Crone of Big Broughton introducing a roll-call that concluded with Samuel Snaith of Cockermouth – coal miner and self-employed property clearance operative. Laid out flat, I kept this vital record stored away inside the opening pages of a dog-eared copy of Chatwin's *On the Black Hill.* Hidden from the sun's eye, and brought out every so often, the names pointed to a final adventure. Some form of nostalgic spell where the dark horizon laments their fate.

00:11

"There was once a dream that was Rome, you could only whisper it, anything more than a whisper and it would vanish, it was so fragile…" (Sir Richard Harris playing the Emperor 'Marcus Aurelius' in the film, *Gladiator*)

It began with a gathering for a so-called 'family photo' at the Eternal City's Trevi Fountain. Flanked on all sides by imposing buildings hollowed out of the honeycomb of stone, the G20 leaders themselves are often regarded like Ancient Romans - lazy, corrupt and bloated, not to be trusted. During this meeting, instead of seeking La Dolce Vita, they must have been wishing for a return to the pre-COVID19 world. A world where Kleptocracy's fall from grace could throw dishonesty over its own shoulders and land it somewhere discreetly out of sight. But with growing concerns over Eco anxiety amid the continuous clouds of corruption, a new form of politics requires trillions of dollars to save the planet for generations yet unborn.

00:12

The melancholy spectacle of a major winter storm greeted the opening of COP26. High winds bringing major disruption to roads and rail services that forced people to abandon journeys to Glasgow, the host city. Climate breakdown caused by trapped heat and rising sea temperatures producing hurricanes and tornados. COP26's ticking clock for a profit-driven planet being wrecked before our eyes. Some kind of sick joke that forced Lord Goldsmith the environment minister, along with many other delegates, to book flights after their trains were held up and cancelled due to trees falling on overhead wires. Extreme weather as the 'new normal'. Taking flights to a climate change conference and flying in the face of the science. From the bleakness of the Covid pandemic to another future doomsday where runaway climate change is inevitable.

In the build-up, a familiar pot called kettle with Boris Johnson warning of 'hollow pledges' on emissions. While national treasure Sir David Attenborough signalled the conference as a moment of 'crisis', with a simple plea for 'bold action' (to halt the burning of fossil fuels), thus replacing Johnson's spoof three-word slogan *Hands, Face, Space*. COP26, yet another 'make-or-break' conference, but this time aiming to mark a shift to the phasing out of coal power, while pledging an extra £1 billion to help vulnerable nations adapt to life without the dark stuff. According to the 'State of the Climate' survey undertaken by the World Meteorological Organisation (WMO), the world's temperature has averaged more than one degree above pre-industrial levels for the past two decades. Justifying this new game of high politics, manicured negotiators responded by rolling out a one-size-fits-all catchphrase, 'Keeping 1.5 Alive!' In a world now 1 degree warmer, honouring the 2015 Paris Agreement target of 1.5 to 2 degrees above pre-industrial levels would ease fears and put everything 'back on track'. Those old world anxieties over nuclear war or the death of religion have been displaced by the climate trauma of unprecedented floods, fires, heatwaves and increasingly extreme weather patterns.

Yet the stark contrast between the mainstream politics of COP26's President Alok *'No Drama'* Sharma and the activist Zoomers led by such prominent young figures as 18 year old Greta Thunberg and 24 year old Malala Yousafzai could not have been bigger. Underselling self-awareness, Sharma in full-on David Brent mode could never hope to match the passionate, fully engaged and committed new radicals aiming to uproot the broken system. Thunberg's *Blah, blah, blah…* sounded a modern day '*Anthem for a Doomed Youth*', a sad bugle call highlighting years of empty promises and the repeated failures of global leaders to address the climate emergency. An increasingly desperate situation made more poignant with the UN's Intergovernmental Panel on Climate Change report at August 2021 that warned of a "Code red" situation for humanity, after botched attempts by successive governments to slash greenhouse gas emissions. With the world heading for a carbon war and drastic action thought to be the only option available, on-going plans to allow the mining of metallurgical coal in West Cumbria brought the UK's leadership of COP26 sharply into focus.

00:13

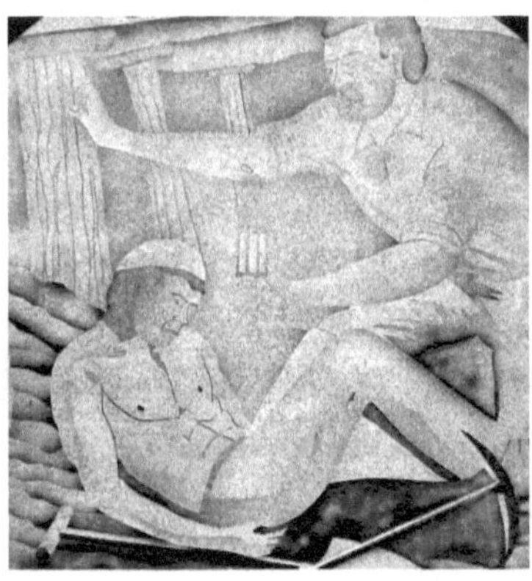

Coal used to mean life and death to Whitehaven, both economically and psychologically. For Sam and his ancestors, it formed a dedicated extraction of the genius loci some 300 years in the making. Initially, I had hoped that researching my father's list of names might provide a deeper understanding of the area where they lived and the kind of lives they must have led. I was wrong. If anything, the mining history and industrial grandeur once associated with West Cumbria has only heightened my curiosity to try and dig deeper. Now it is clear to me that my ancestors were guided by a shared view rooted in the wisdom of survival. They inhabited a world of darkened skies driven by consumption with the extraction and burning of fossil fuels that was illuminated by living coals with pink mists rising and the dark hardened into a wall. In a free economy, the invisible hands of individual demand exported costs both to others and to future generations. Changing the behaviour of fossil fuel addicts after hundreds of years of reliance has often been compared to weaning a junkie off drugs.

Saving the planet to get to a clean and nature-rich environment makes contemplating a new mine in today's war torn economic and social fabric an undoubtedly difficult decision. This controversial proposal has already succeeded in reopening familiar old wounds. Extracting around 2.8 million tonnes from both onshore and offshore seams every year for around 50 years, coal that will be metallurgical-grade for use in both the UK and Europe. *Coal for Steel.* On track to supply UK steelmaking coal. And with the UK's diminished worldwide reputation even more at risk, COP26 applied the brakes to the decision to open the mine. After all, they couldn't just let it sneak through with a nudge and a wink. Protecting the biosphere amid mounting concerns. The mutual dependencies of consumer capitalism cannot Keep 1.5 Alive if nature takes over and more forests burn as the sea ice melts. Optimism versus realism. Now more than ever, we need leaders who can listen to the scientists and who are responsible enough to take care of the planet.

00:14

Reactions to COP26 were mixed. George Monbiot, a passionate advocate for social and ecological justice, called the Glasgow climate pact, a 'pathetic, limp rag of a document'. Despite a declaration approved by nearly 200 hundred nations after two weeks of talks, most researchers could only express a collective relief that any sort of agreement had been reached. Others left the meeting frustrated at the lack of stronger commitments to reduce emissions, coupled with a failure to agree so-called "loss and damage" finance for countries that are most vulnerable to climate change. Various activists dismissed the pact as a betrayal; UN Secretary-General António Guterres spoke of 'emergency modes' while US climate envoy John Kerry cautiously welcomed a set of good compromises that left everyone slightly unsatisfied. Greta Thunberg's *"Blah, blah, blah…"* dismissed both the deal and the last minute U-turn entirely. Predictably, it was the old dark stuff that caused the biggest controversy after a last-minute change watered down a crucial piece of language. The revision to the wording of the text, promoted by India and backed by China, called for nations to "phase *down*" rather than "phase *out*" use of the dirtiest fossil fuel. A final outcome that prompted Jennifer Morgan, executive director of Greenpeace International, to issue a guarded warning aimed at lobbyists from the oil and gas industry, "They changed a word but they can't change the signal coming out of this COP that the era of coal is ending. If you're a coal company executive, this COP saw a bad outcome. "It's in the interests of all countries, including those who still burn coal, to transition to clean renewable energy, and richer countries need to do more to support the shift. Our future depends on it."

00:15

The battle lines have long been drawn in the global conflict between environmentalists and the producers of fossil fuels. Often seen as nothing more than just a big carbon headache, coal is undoubtedly proving to be a hard habit to break. In energy hungry nations across Asia, new coal-fired power plants are being switched on every year. Providing more than a third of global electricity the main issues surrounding its continued use are often simplified down to this, burgeoning consumption versus carbon reduction. At the beginning of October 2021, after plans for the mine put forward by WCM had been called-in by the Secretary of State, a planning inspector concluded a 16-day public inquiry. The final call on whether to approve the mine, based on the findings of the inquiry, is set to be announced late 2022. Whatever the decision, it will mark a turning point in the ongoing debate surrounding fossil fuels. With guaranteed hostility at the outcome from both sides of the carbon war, the resulting implications will be felt locally for decades to come.

00:16

Heading past a string of car dealerships on a long, straight section of the A595 to Whitehaven, I got stuck behind a *Mad Max* type patrolling the West Cumbrian badlands on a smooth and powerful Honda Gold Wing. The night time ritual of survival for a road warrior reduced to scraps and shreds in a fuel-injected suicide machine.

From memory to myth, my father's glazed face in my own, travelling towards a new story-time with a moving rubber belt carrying a glittering river of coal. Reflected off the passenger window, a clamour of rooks in a frozen field formed a rough circle. In the middle, a pair with rakish eyes and grey-white faces chatted away hoarsely to each other. Singing to scattered ghosts, a gradual darkness overtook the ground. In the dying fires the clock summoned us.

While the alluring dark grasp of earth smiled back from the Irish Sea...